HAL•LEONARD

BASS PLAY•ALONG

VOL. 14

MODERN ROCK

ISBN 978-1-4234-1427-8

HAL•LEONARD®
CORPORATION
7777 W. BLUEMOUND RD. P.O. BOX 13819 MILWAUKEE, WI 53213

Visit Hal Leonard Online at
www.halleonard.com

HAL•LEONARD

BASS
PLAY•ALONG™

VOL. 14

MODERN
ROCK

CONTENTS

Bass Notation Legend

Bass music can be notated two different ways: on a musical staff, and in tablature

THE MUSICAL STAFF shows pitches and rhythms and is divided by bar lines into measures. Pitches are named after the first seven letters of the alphabet.

TABLATURE graphically represents the bass fingerboard. Each horizontal line represents a string, and each number represents a fret.

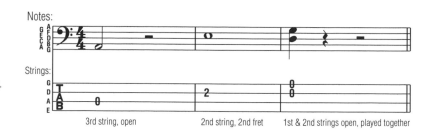

Notes:

Strings:

3rd string, open   2nd string, 2nd fret   1st & 2nd strings open, played together

HAMMER-ON: Strike the first (lower) note with one finger, then sound the higher note (on the same string) with another finger by fretting it without picking.

PULL-OFF: Place both fingers on the notes to be sounded. Strike the first note and without picking, pull the finger off to sound the second (lower) note.

LEGATO SLIDE: Strike the first note and then slide the same fret-hand finger up or down to the second note. The second note is not struck.

SHIFT SLIDE: Same as legato slide, except the second note is struck.

TRILL: Very rapidly alternate between the notes indicated by continuously hammering on and pulling off.

TREMOLO PICKING: The note is picked as rapidly and continuously as possible.

VIBRATO: The string is vibrated by rapidly bending and releasing the note with the fretting hand.

SHAKE: Using one finger, rapidly alternate between two notes on one string by sliding either a half-step above or below.

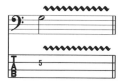

NATURAL HARMONIC: Strike the note while the fret hand lightly touches the string directly over the fret indicated.

Harm.

MUFFLED STRINGS: A percussive sound is produced by laying the fret hand across the string(s) without depressing them and striking them with the pick hand.

BEND: Strike the note and bend up the interval shown.

1/2

BEND AND RELEASE: Strike the note and bend up as indicated, then release back to the original note. Only the first note is struck.

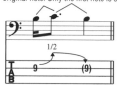

1/2

RIGHT-HAND TAP: Hammer ("tap") the fret indicated with the "pick-hand" index or middle finger and pull off to the note fretted by the fret hand.

LEFT-HAND TAP: Hammer ("tap") the fret indicated with the "fret-hand" index or middle finger.

SLAP: Strike ("slap") string with right-hand thumb.

POP: Snap ("pop") string with right-hand index or middle finger.

Additional Musical Definitions

(accent)

• Accentuate note (play it louder)

(accent)

• Accentuate note with great intensity

(staccato)

• Play the note short

D.S. al Coda

• Go back to the sign (𝄋), then play until the measure marked *"To Coda"*, then skip to the section labelled *"Coda."*

Fill

• Label used to identify a brief pattern which is to be inserted into the arrangement.

• Repeat measures between signs.

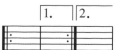

• When a repeated section has different endings, play the first ending only the first time and the second ending only the second time.

Aerials

Words and Music by Daron Malakian and Serj Tankian

Drop D tuning, down 1 step:
(low to high) C-G-C-F

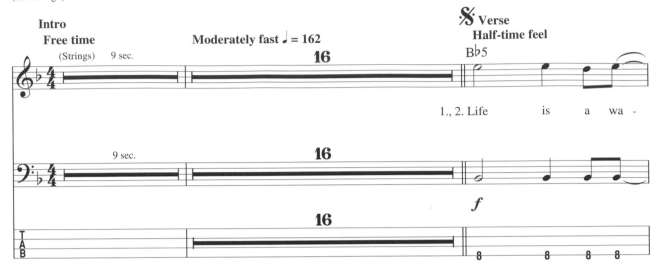

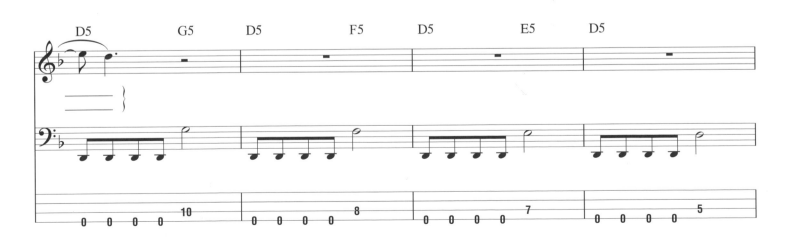

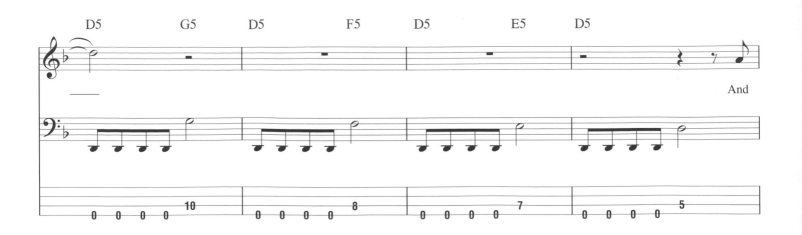

And

To Coda ⊕

we are the ones that wan - - na choose, ___ al - ways wan - na play but you nev - er wan - na lose. _____

Interlude

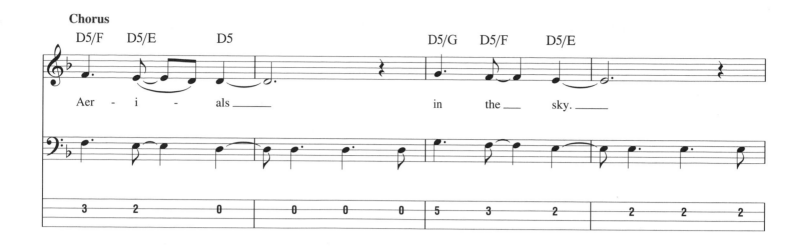

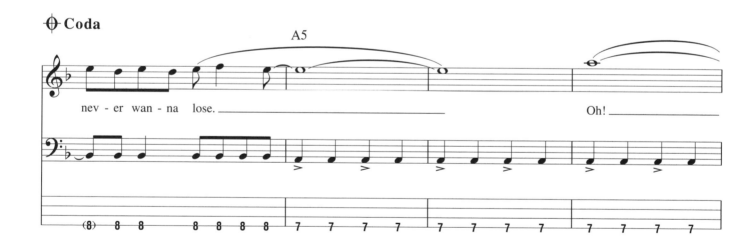

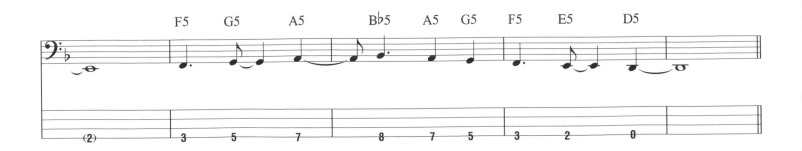

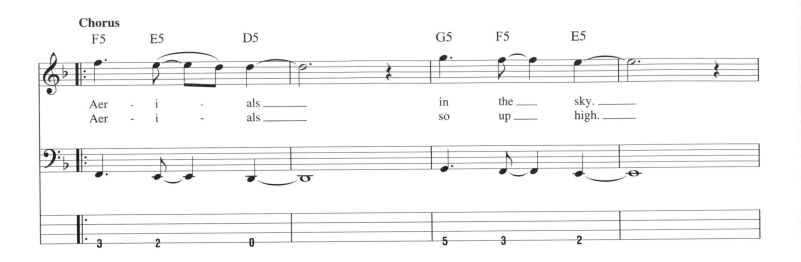

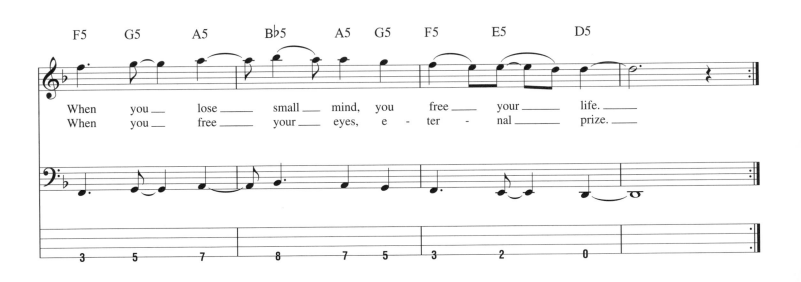

When you __ lose __ small __ mind, you __ free __ your __ life. __
When you __ free __ your __ eyes, e - ter - nal __ prize. __

Outro

Ah, _____ ah. _____

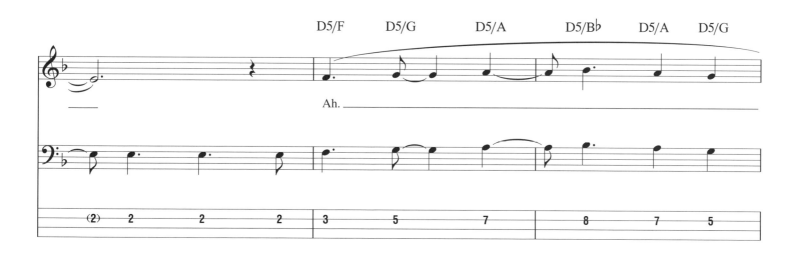

__ Ah. _____

Duality

Words and Music by M. Shawn Crahan, Paul Gray, Nathan Jordison, Corey Taylor, James Root and Sid Wilson

Drop D tuning, down 1 1/2 steps:
(low to high) B-F#-B-E

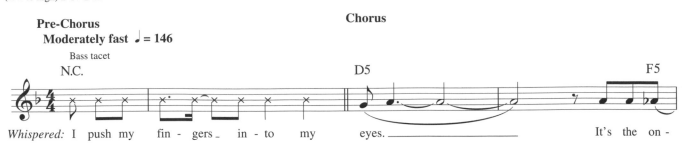

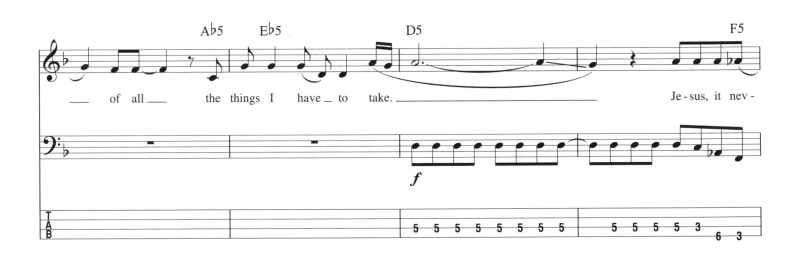

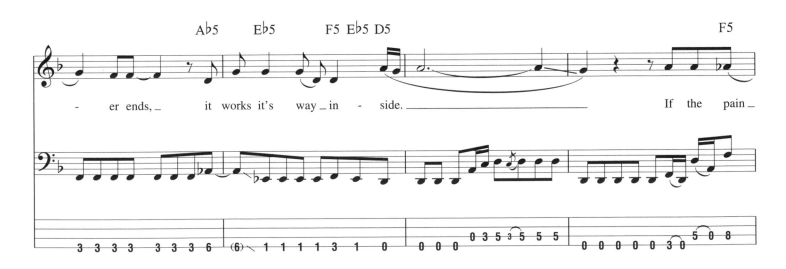

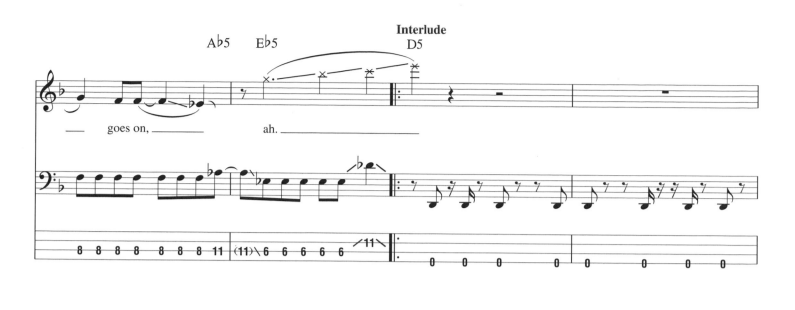

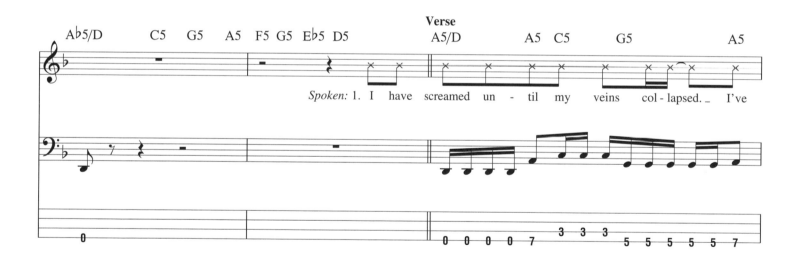

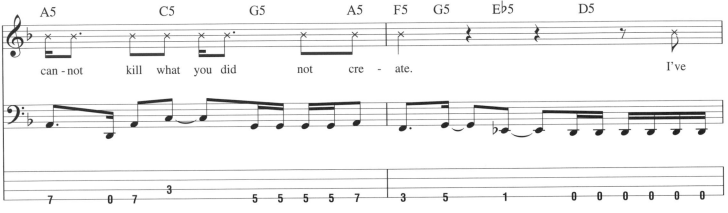

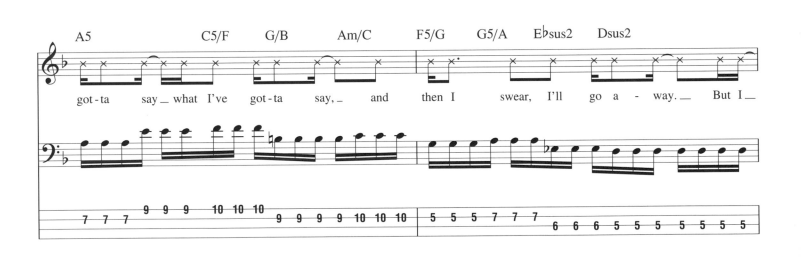

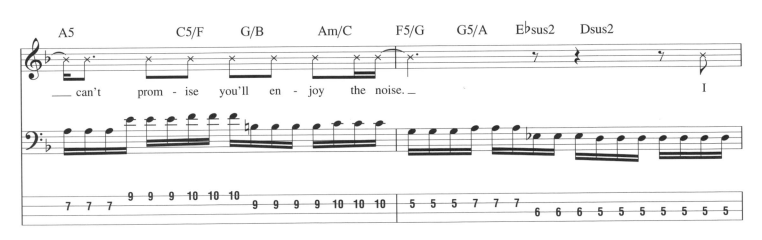

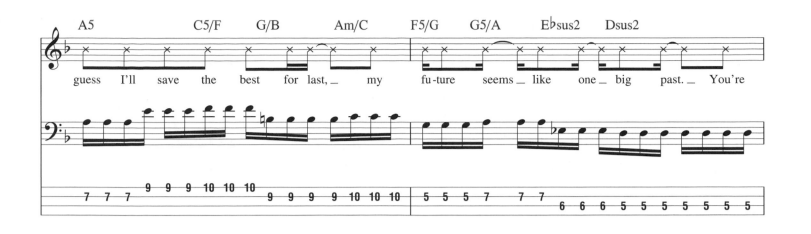

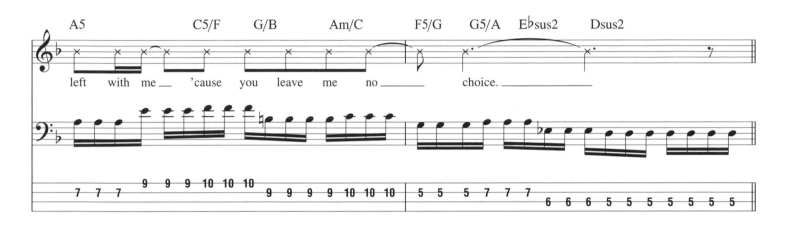

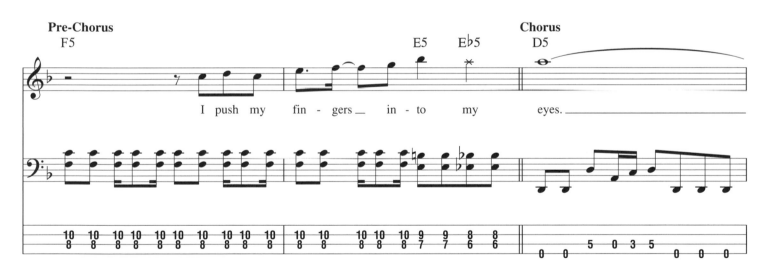

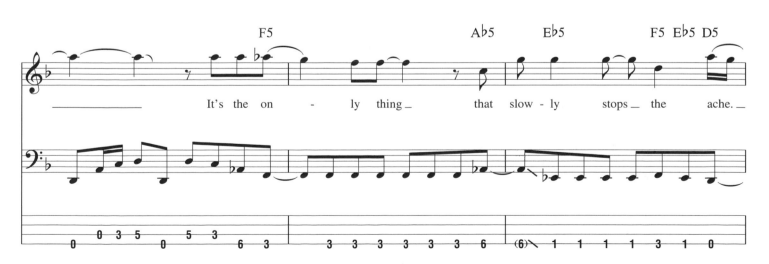

If the pain ___ goes on. ___ I'm not gon - na make it.

Interlude

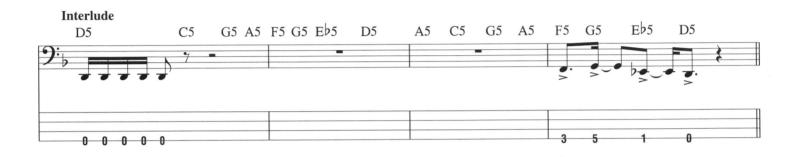

Verse

Spoken: 2. Put me back to-geth - er, or sep - a - rate ___ the skin from bone.

Leave me all the piec - es, then you can ___ leave me a - lone. ___

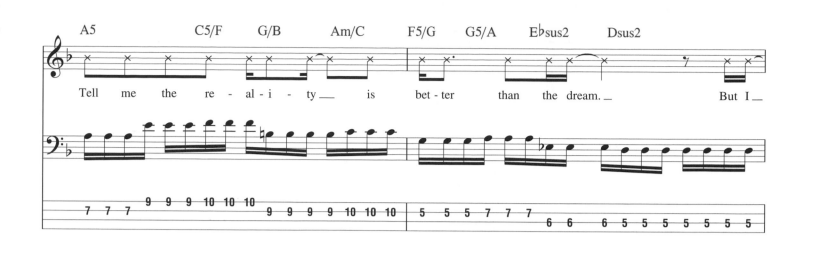

A5   C5/F   G/B   Am/C   F5/G   G5/A   E♭sus2   Dsus2

Tell me the re - al - i - ty __ is bet - ter than the dream. __ But I __

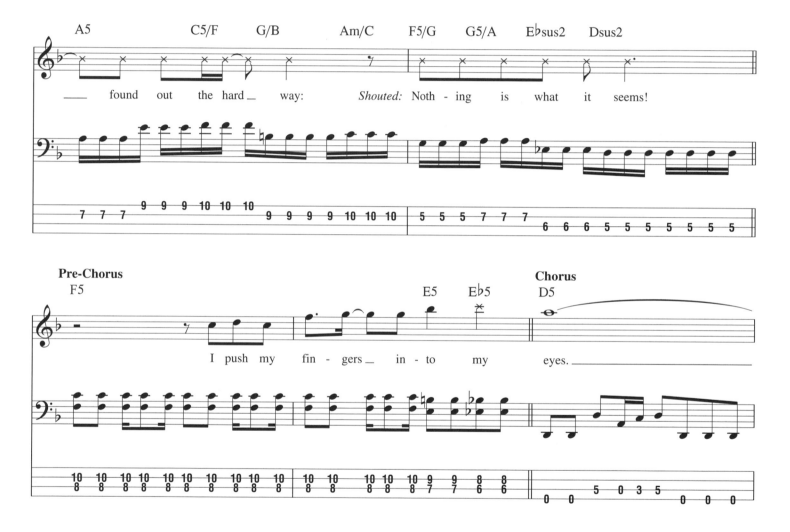

A5   C5/F   G/B   Am/C   F5/G   G5/A   E♭sus2   Dsus2

__ found out the hard __ way: *Shouted:* Noth - ing is what it seems!

Pre-Chorus

F5   E5   E♭5   **Chorus** D5

I push my fin - gers __ in - to my eyes. _____

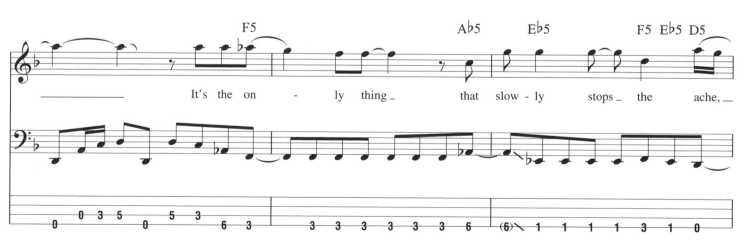

F5   A♭5   E♭5   F5 E♭5 D5

___ It's the on - ly thing __ that slow - ly stops __ the ache, __

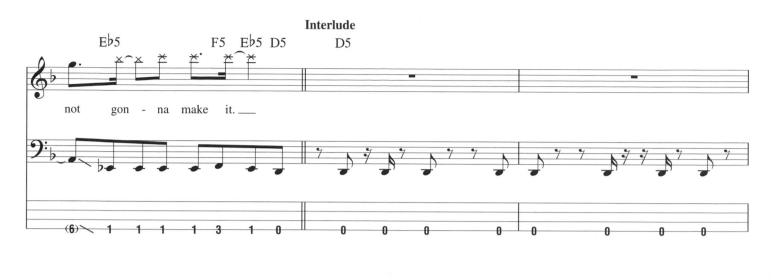

not gon - na make it. ___

Interlude

Bridge
Half-time feel

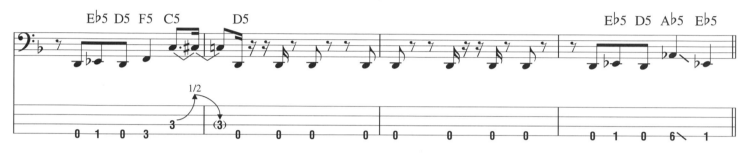

Spoken: All I've got, all ___

___ I've got is in - sane. ___ All I've got, all ___

19

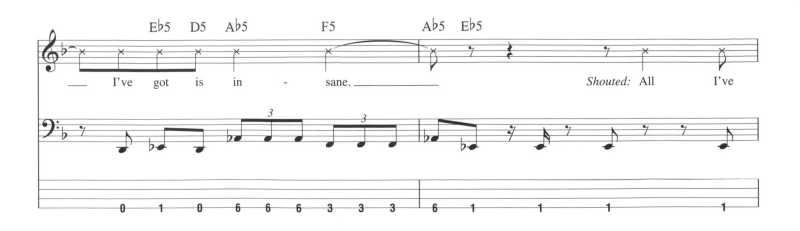

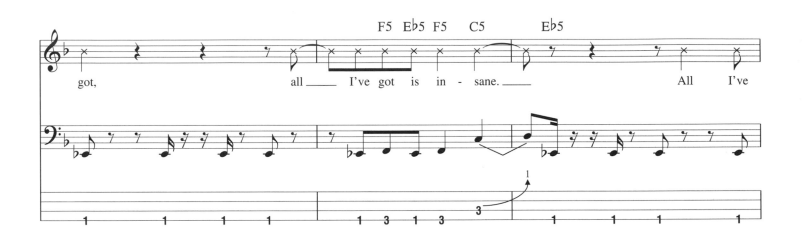

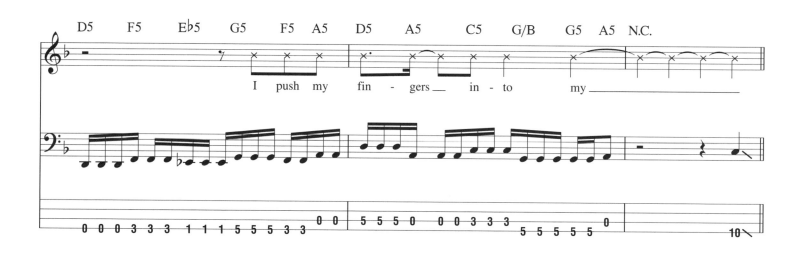

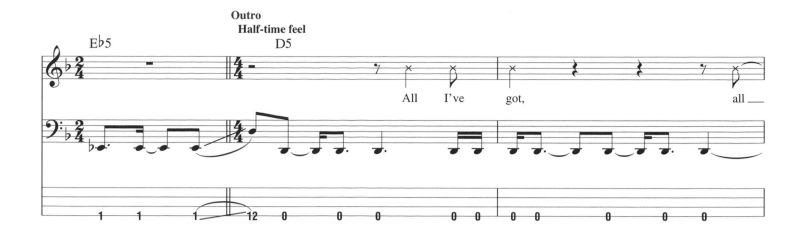

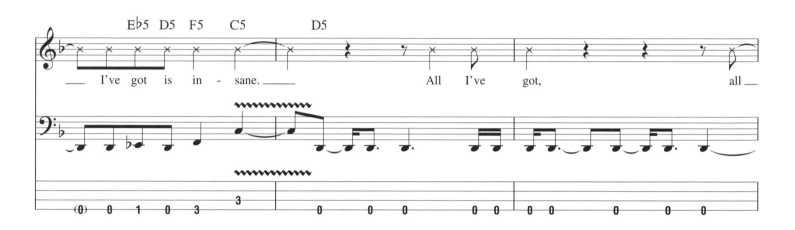

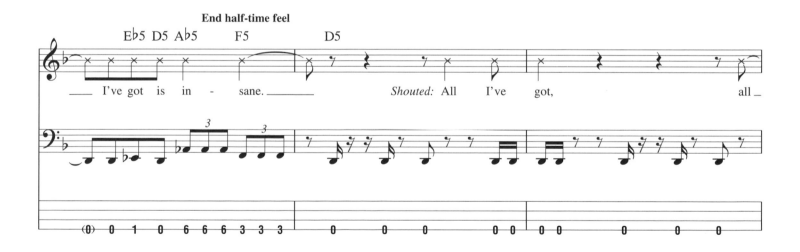

Here to Stay

Words and Music by Jonathan Davis, James Shaffer, Brian Welch, Reginald Arvizu and David Silveria

5-string bass, tune down 1 step:
(low to high) A-D-G-C-F

Intro
Moderately ♩ = 102

1. This time I'm tak-ing it a-way, I've got a prob-lem
2. *See additional lyrics*

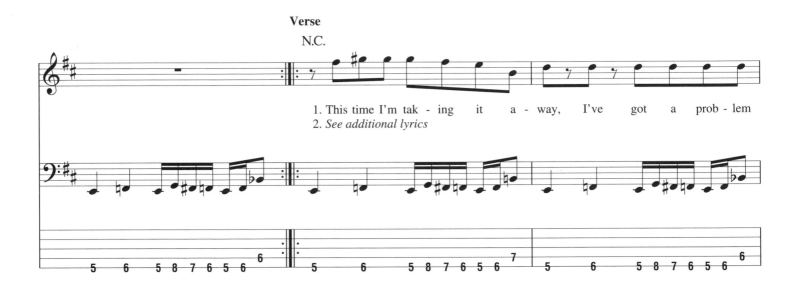

with me get-ting in the way, my vi-'lent side. So, I take my face and

% Pre-Chorus

N.C.

This pain is el - e - vat - ing as the hurt turns in - to hat - ing,

an - tic - i - pat - ing all the fucked - up feel - ings a - gain.

Chorus

The hurt in - side is fad - ing, this shit's gone way too far. All this time I've been wait - ing.

D.S. al Coda

Coda

Outro

N.C.

Play 4 times

Give an - y - more.

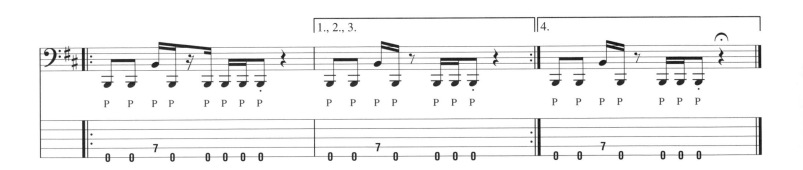

Additional Lyrics

2. My mind's done with this. Okay, I've got a question.
   Can I throw it all away? Take back what's mine.
   So I take my time, guiding the blade down the line.
   Each cut closer to the vein. Bleed! Bleed!

Judith

Words and Music by Maynard James Keenan and Billy Howerdel

Tune down 1 1/2 steps:
(low to high) C#-F#-B-E

Intro

Moderately fast Rock ♩. = 55

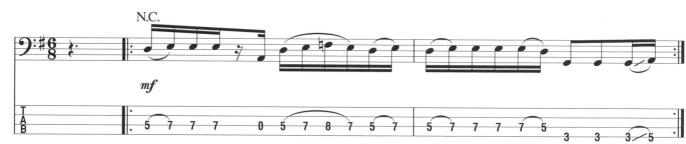

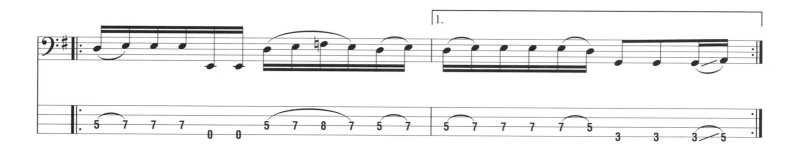

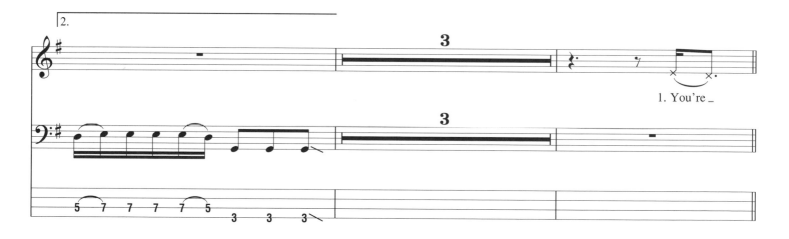

Verse

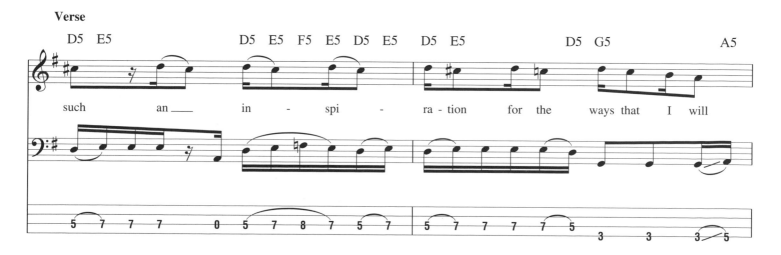

such an __ in - spi - ra - tion for the ways that I will

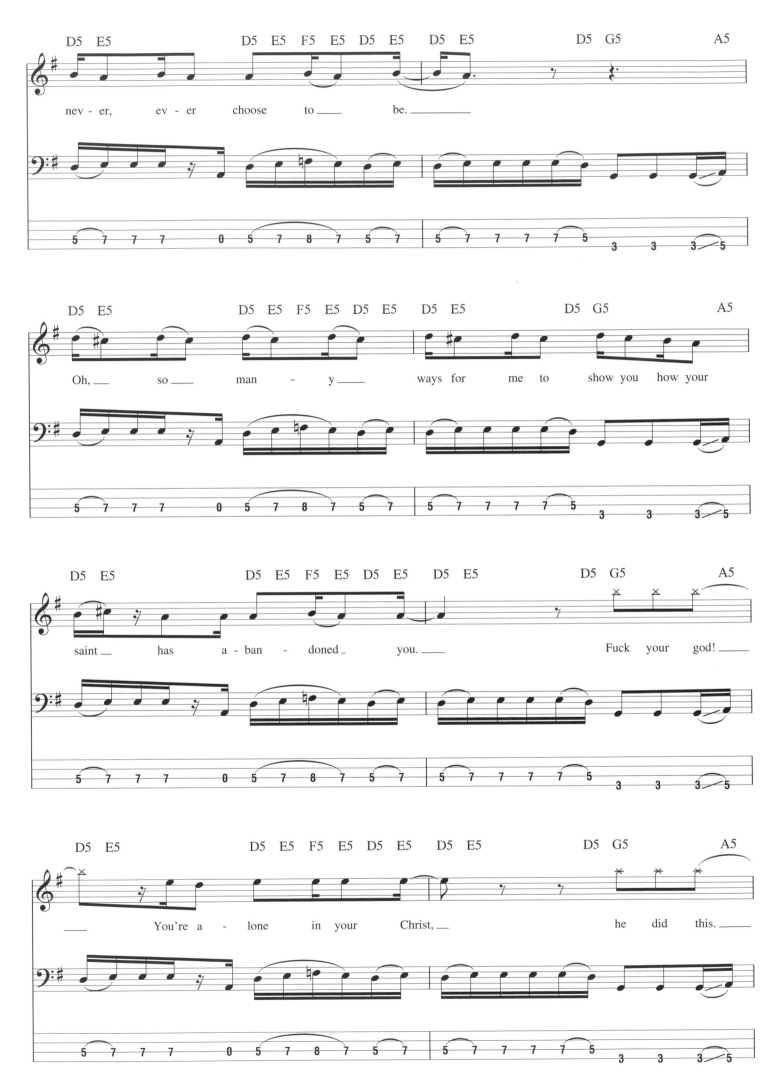

2nd time, substitute Fill 1

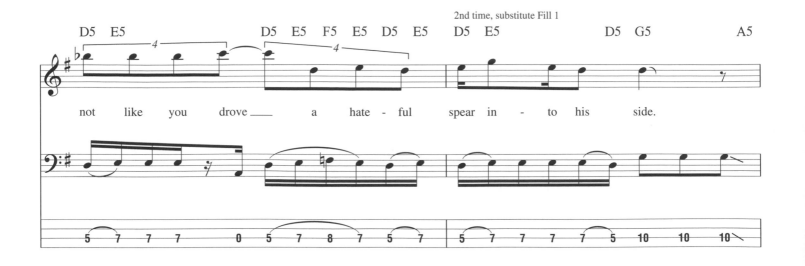

not like you drove ___ a hate-ful spear in-to his side.

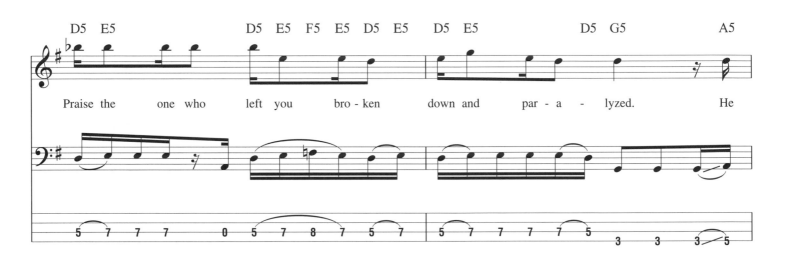

Praise the one who left you bro-ken down and par-a-lyzed. He

To Coda ⊕

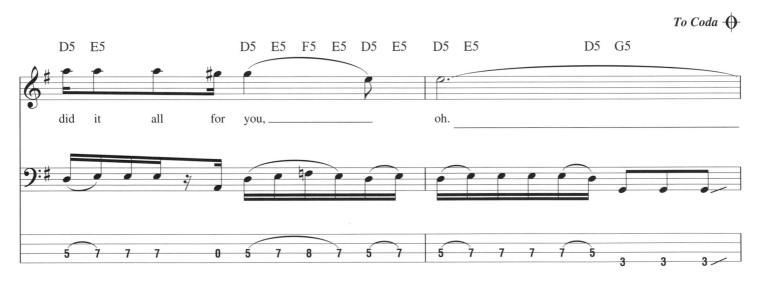

did it all for you, _____ oh. _____

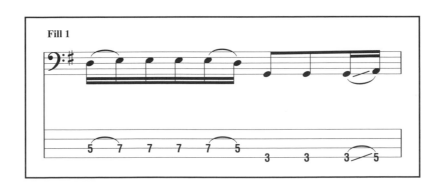

Fill 1

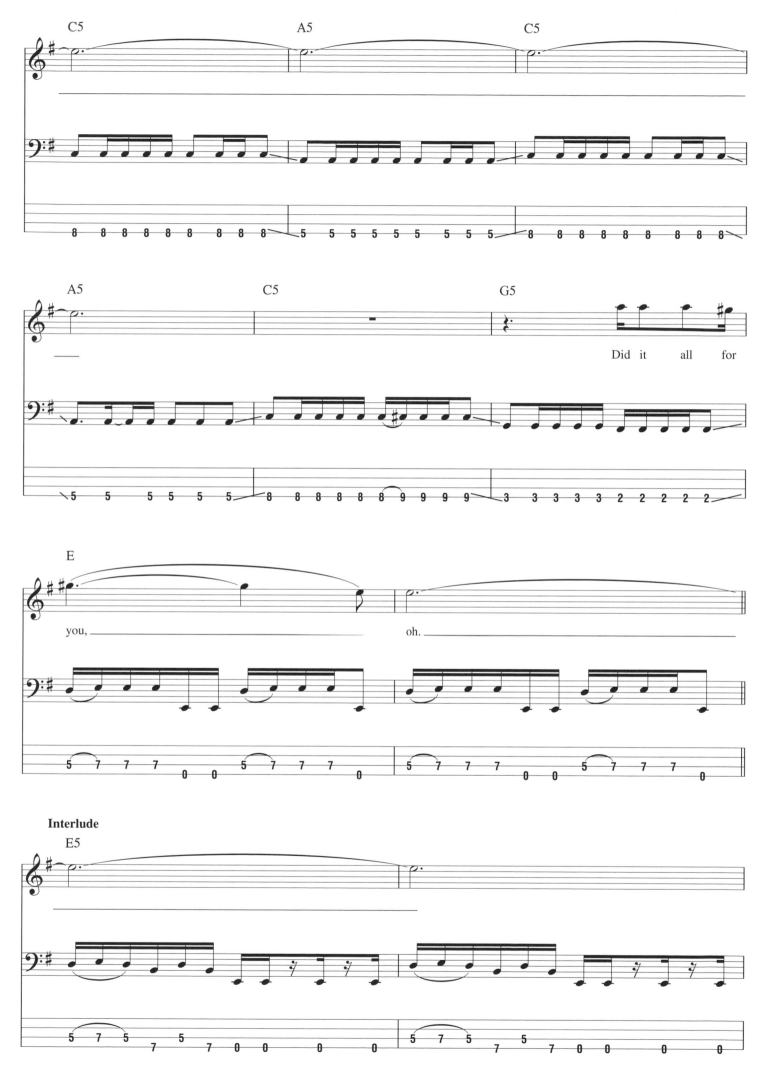

D5

Play 4 times

Verse

E5

2. Oh, so __ man - y __ ways for me to show you how your

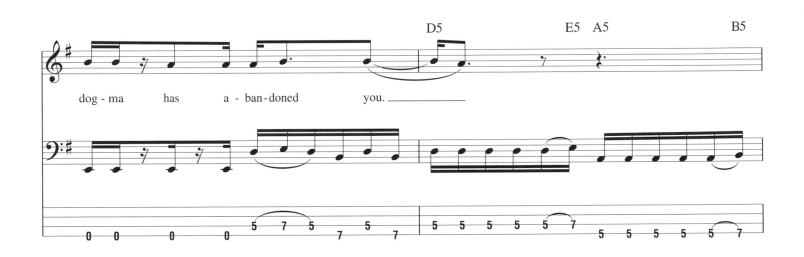

D5   E5   A5   B5

dog - ma has a - ban - doned you. _____

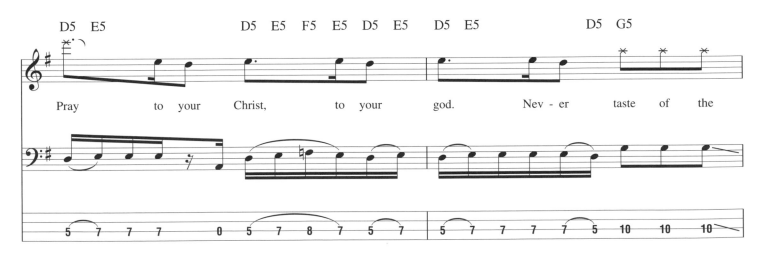

D5   E5   D5   E5   F5   E5   D5   E5   D5   E5   D5   G5

Pray to your Christ, to your god. Nev - er taste of the

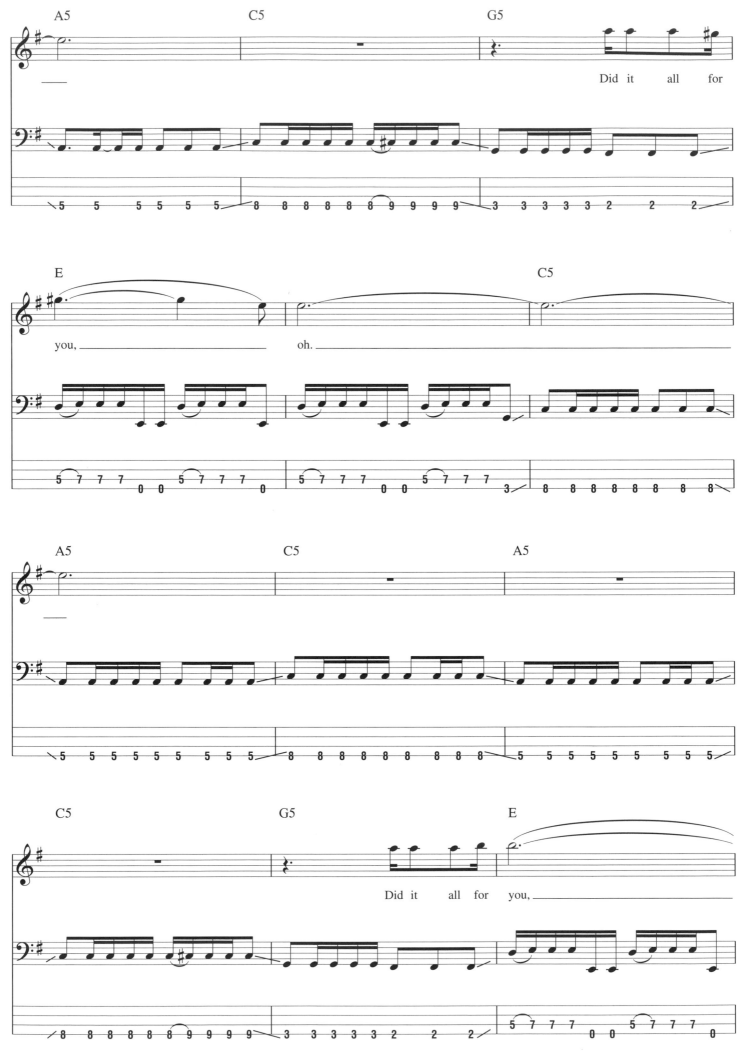

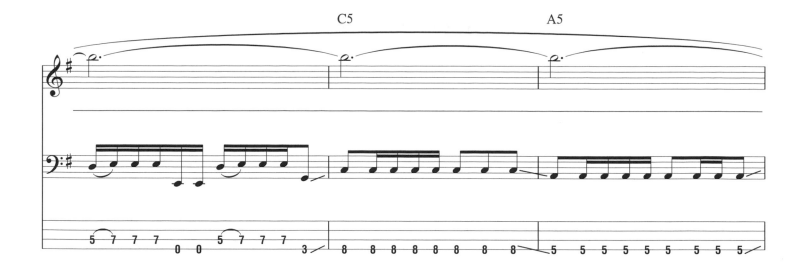

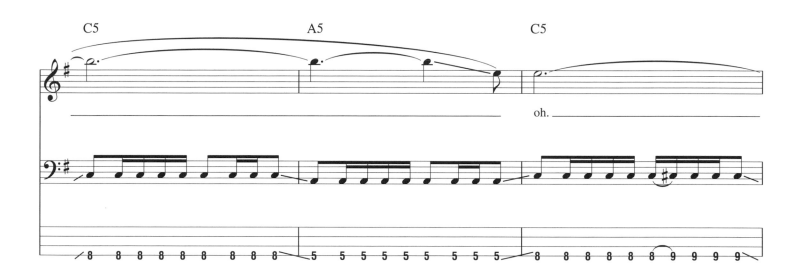

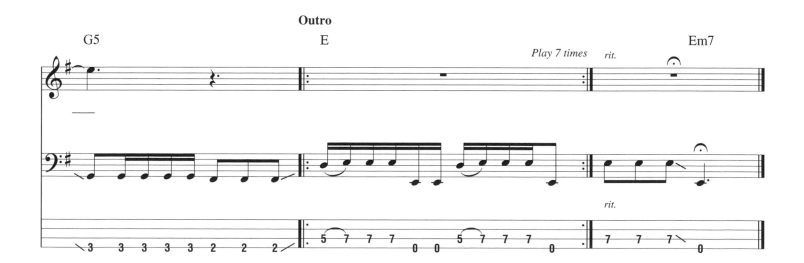

Additional Lyrics

Chorus   Not like you killed someone.
It's not like you drove a spiteful spear into his side.
Talk to Jesus Christ as if he knows the reasons why.
He did it all for you, oh. Did it all for you, oh.

I Stand Alone

Words and Music by Sully Erna

Drop D tuning, down 1 step:
(low to high) C-G-C-F

Intro
Moderately slow ♩ = 84

1. I've told _____ you this one _____ be - fore, _____ can't con - trol me.
2. *See additional lyrics*

If you _____ try to _____ take me down you're gon - na break.

Chorus

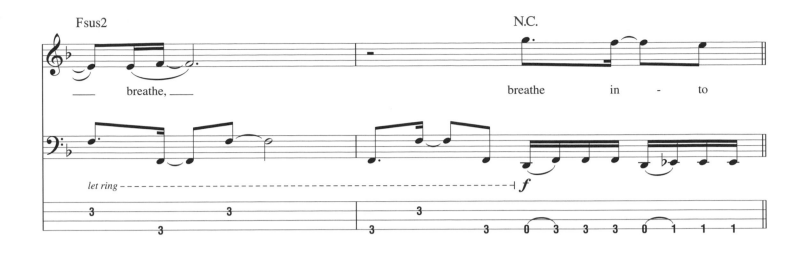

breathe, breathe in - to

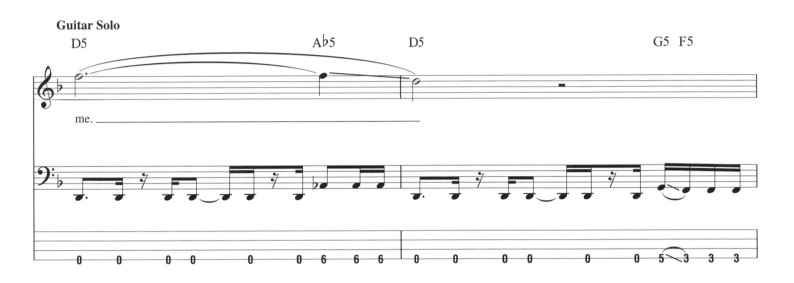

Guitar Solo

me.

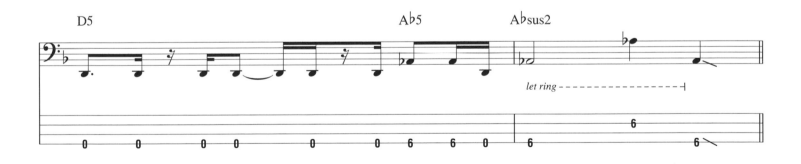

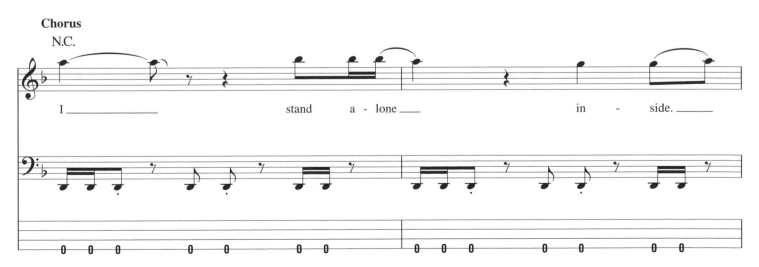

Chorus

N.C.

I stand a - lone in - side.

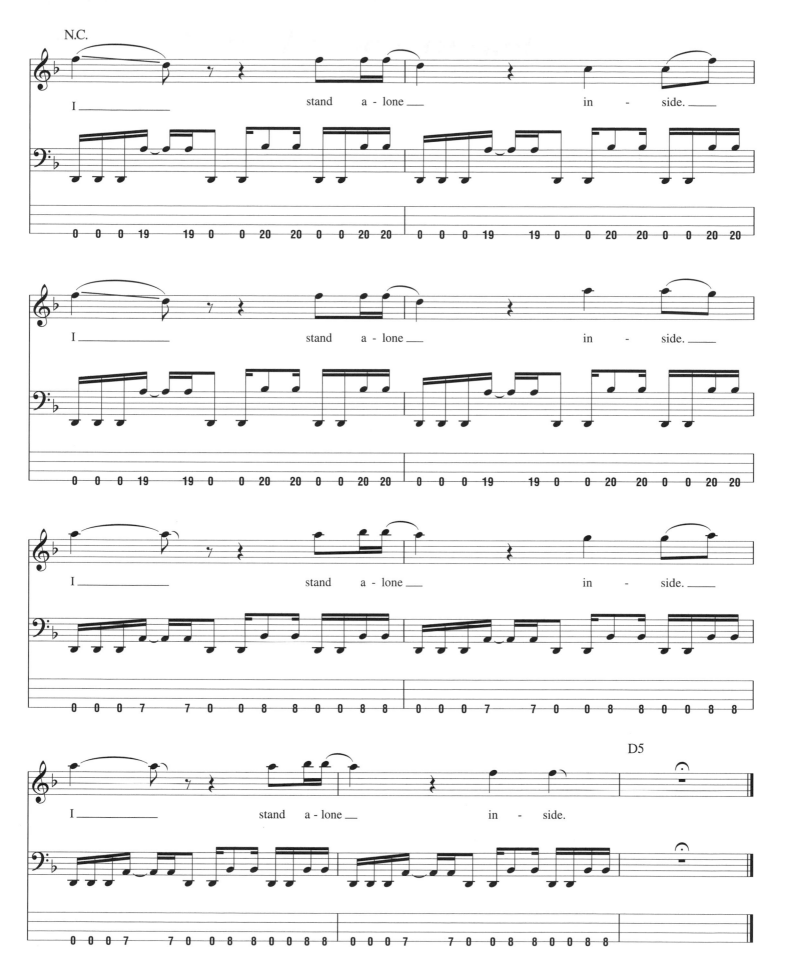

Additional Lyrics

2. You're always hiding behind your so-called goddess.
So what? You don't think that we can see your face?
Resurrected back before the final falling.
And I'll never rest until I can make my own way.
I'm not afraid of fading.

Nice to Know You

Words and Music by Brandon Boyd, Michael Einziger, Alex Katunich, Jose Pasillas II and Chris Kilmore

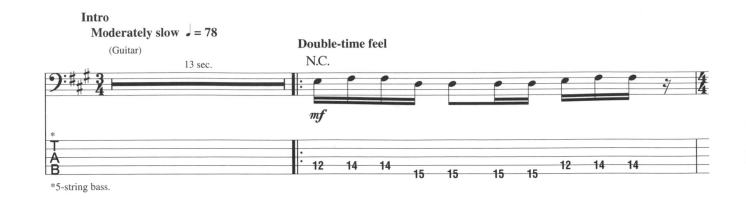

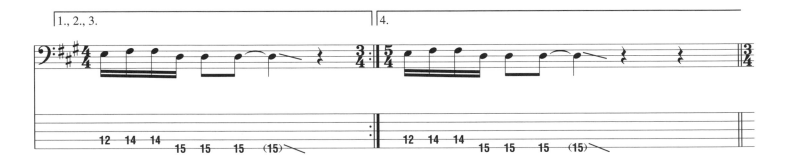

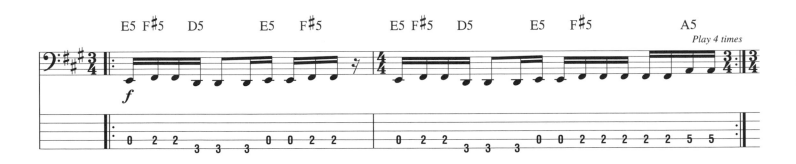

1. Bet - ter than watch - ing Gel - ler bend - ing sil - ver ___ spoons.
2. *See additional lyrics*

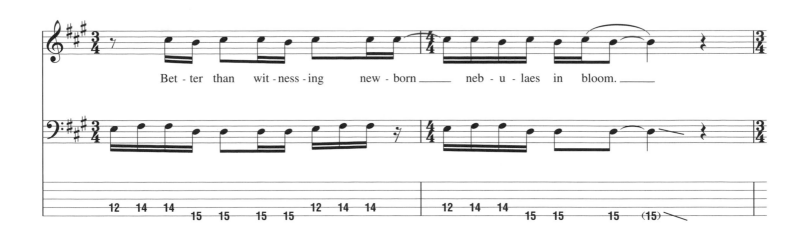

Bet -ter than wit -ness -ing new - born _____ neb - u - laes in bloom. _____

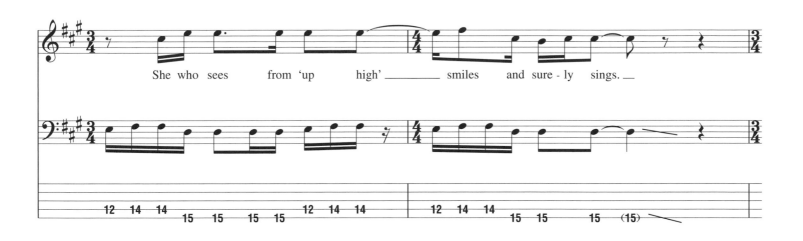

She who sees from 'up high' _____ smiles and sure - ly sings. __

End double-time feel

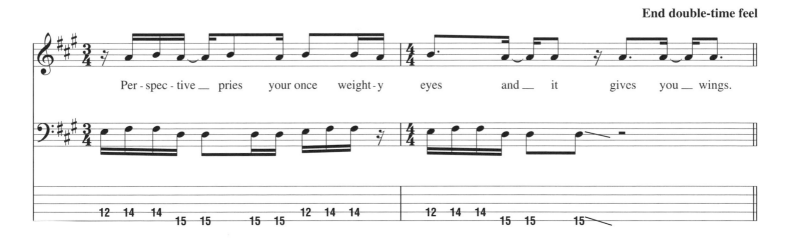

Per - spec - tive __ pries your once weight - y eyes and __ it gives you __ wings.

%**Pre-Chorus**

Asus2   Amaj7sus2

I have - n't felt _____ the way I feel to - day __

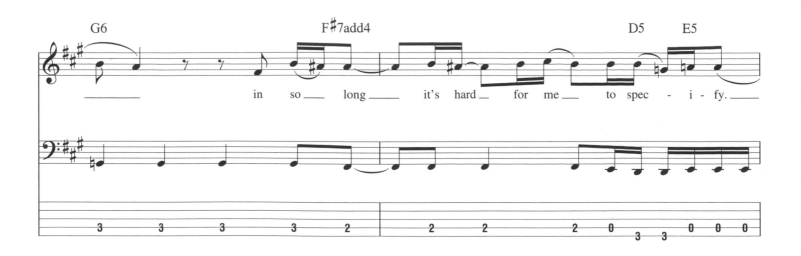

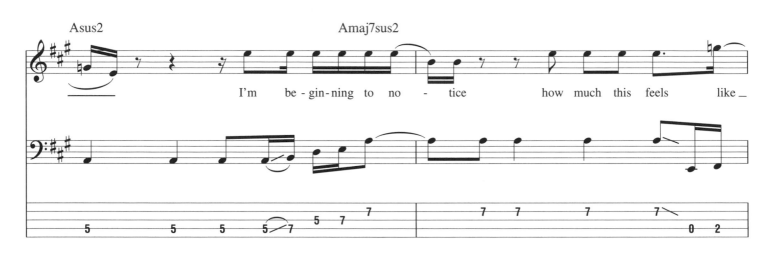

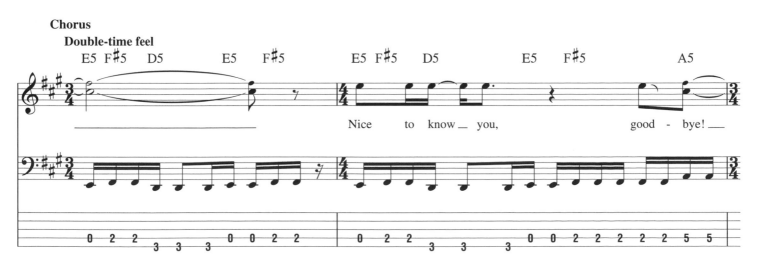

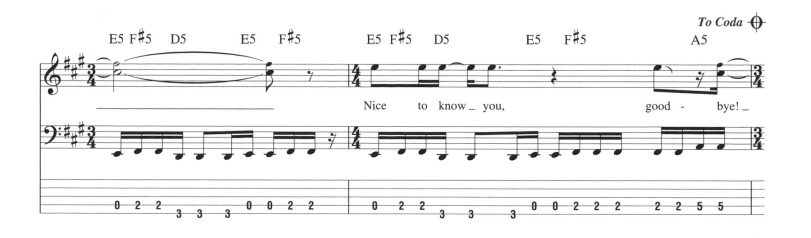

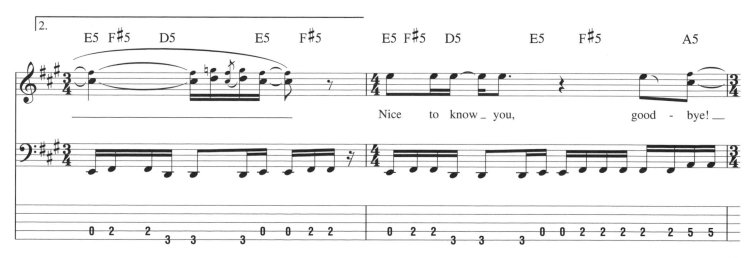

Bridge

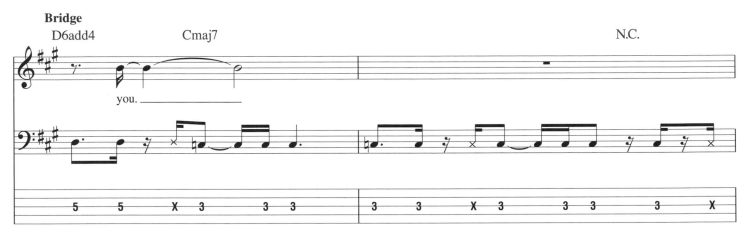

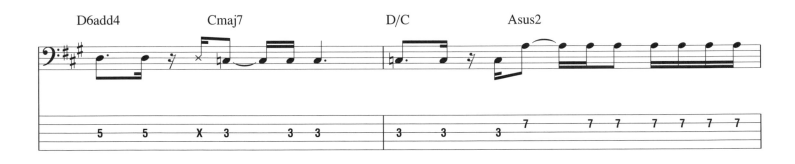

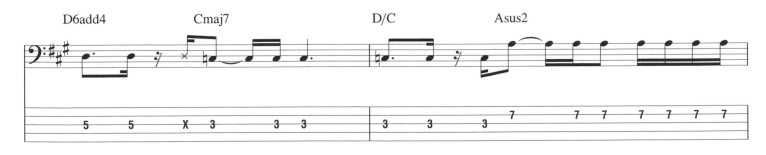

D.S. al Coda

Additional Lyrics

2. Deeper than the deepest Cousteau would ever go.
   And higher than the heights of what we often think we know.
   Blessed she who clearly sees the wood for the trees.
   To obtain a "bird's eye" is to turn a blizzard to a breeze.

Nookie

Words and Music by Fred Durst, Wesley Borland, Sam Rivers, John Otto and Leor Dimant

Tune down 1 1/2 steps:
(low to high) C#-F#-B-E

Intro
Moderate Rock ♩ = 98

Check, one, one, two. 1. I

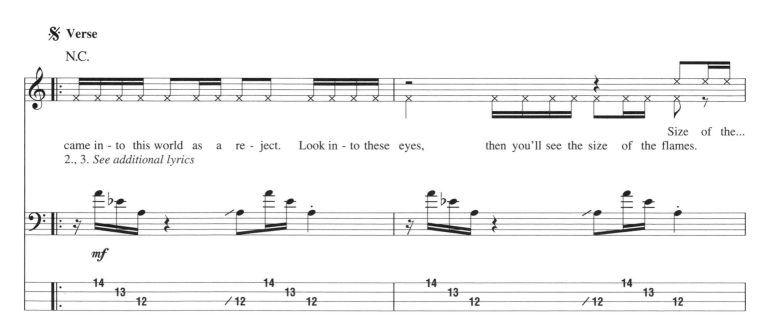

came in-to this world as a re-ject. Look in-to these eyes, then you'll see the size of the flames.
2., 3. *See additional lyrics*

Size of the...

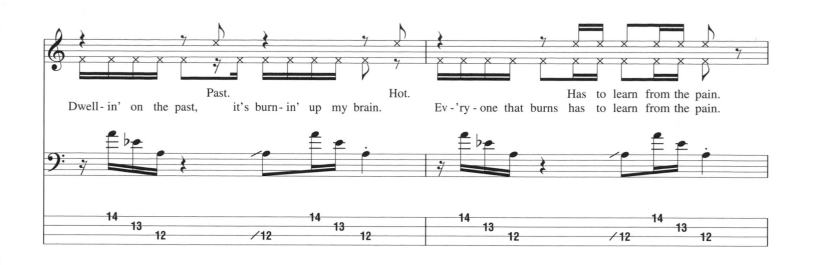

Dwell-in' on the past, it's burn-in' up my brain. Ev-'ry-one that burns has to learn from the pain.

Past. Hot. Has to learn from the pain.

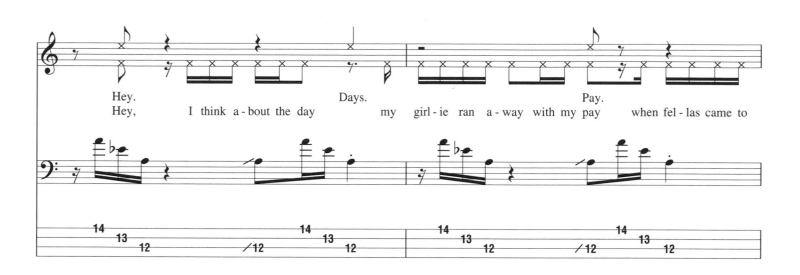

Hey, I think a-bout the day my girl-ie ran a-way with my pay when fel-las came to

Hey. Days. Pay.

To Coda 1 ⊕

Play.
play. Now she's stuck with my hom-ies that she fucked, and I'm just a suck-er with a lump in my

Ooh.

1.

Bass tacet

throat like a chump, like a chump, like a chump, like a

Hey, hey, hey, hey,

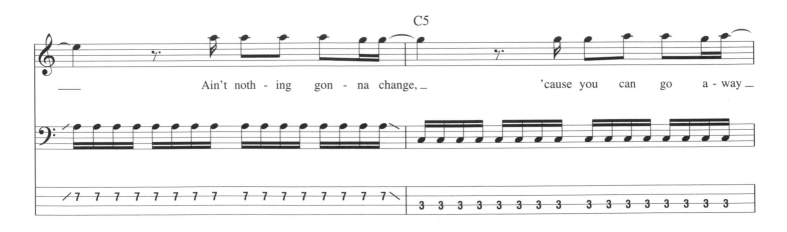

C5

Ain't noth-ing gon-na change,___ 'cause you can go a-way___

D.S.S. al Coda 3
(take repeat)

D5   E5   G5

and I'm just gon-na stay ___ here and al-ways be the same.___

 Coda 3

Outro

N.C.

Repeat and fade

Additional Lyrics

2. Should I be feelin' bad? (No.) Should I be feelin' good? (No.)
   It's kinda sad, I'm the laughin' stock of the neighborhood.
   And you would think that I'd be movin' on, (Movin'.)
   But I'm a sucker like I said, fucked up in the head. (Not.)
   And maybe she just made a mistake and I should give her a break.
   My heart'll ache either way.
   Hey, what the hell. What you want me to say?
   I won't lie, that I can't deny.

3. Why did it take so long?
   Why did I wait so long, huh, to figure it out?
   But I didn't and I'm the only one underneath the sun who didn't get it.
   I can't believe that I could be deceived (But you were.)
   By my so-called girl, but in reality had a hidden agenda.
   She put my tender heart in a blender, and still I surrendered.
   (Hey,) like a chump, (hey,) like a chump,
   (Hey,) like a chump, (hey,) like a chump,
   (Hey,) like a chump, (hey,) like a chump,
   (Hey,) like a chump.

One Step Closer

Words and Music by Rob Bourdon, Brad Delson, Joe Hahn, Mike Shinoda and Charles Bennington

Drop D tuning, down 1/2 step:
(low to high) Db-Ab-Db-Gb

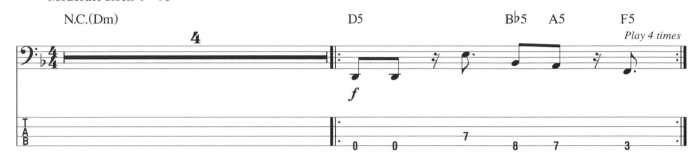

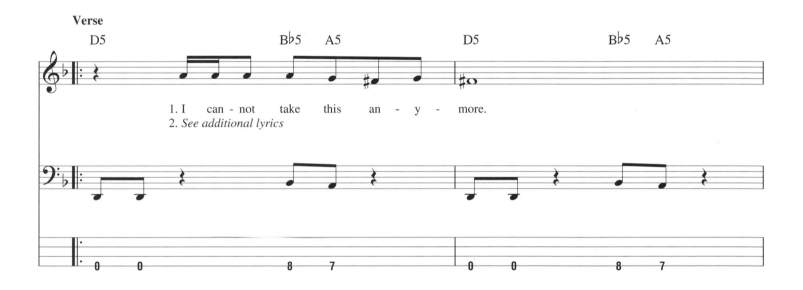

Additional Lyrics

2. I find the answers aren't so clear.
   Wish I could find a way to disappear.
   All these thoughts, they make no sense;
   I find bliss in ignorance.
   Nothing seems to go away; over and over again.
   Just like before...

HAL•LEONARD BASS PLAY•ALONG

The Bass Play-Along Series will help you play your favorite songs quickly and easily! Just follow the tab, listen to the CD to hear how the bass should sound, and then play along using the separate backing tracks. The melody and lyrics are also included in the book in case you want to sing, or to simply help you follow along. The CD is enhanced so you can use your computer to adjust the recording to any tempo without changing pitch!

1. Rock
Songs: Another One Bites the Dust • Badge • Brown Eyed Girl • Come Together • The Joker • Low Rider • Money • Sweet Emotion.
00699674 Book/CD Pack.............. $12.95

2. R&B
Songs: Get Ready • I Can't Help Myself (Sugar Pie, Honey Bunch) • I Got You (I Feel Good) • I Heard It Through the Grapevine • I Want You Back • In the Midnight Hour • My Girl • You Can't Hurry Love.
00699675 Book/CD Pack.............. $12.95

3. Pop/Rock
Songs: Crazy Little Thing Called Love • Crocodile Rock • Maneater • My Life • No Reply at All • Peg • Message in a Bottle • Suffragette City.
00699677 Book/CD Pack.............. $12.95

4. '90s Rock
Songs: All I Wanna Do • Fly Away • Give It Away • Hard to Handle • Jeremy • Know Your Enemy • Spiderwebs • You Oughta Know.
00699679 Book/CD Pack.............. $12.95

5. Funk
Songs: Brick House • Cissy Strut • Get Off • Get Up (I Feel Like Being) a Sex Machine • Higher Ground • Le Freak • Pick up the Pieces • Super Freak.
00699680 Book/CD Pack.............. $12.95

6. Classic Rock
Songs: Free Ride • Funk #49 • Gimme Three Steps • Green-Eyed Lady • Radar Love • Werewolves of London • White Room • Won't Get Fooled Again.
00699678 Book/CD Pack.............. $12.95

7. Hard Rock
Songs: Crazy Train • Detroit Rock City • Iron Man • Livin' on a Prayer • Living After Midnight • Peace Sells • Smoke on the Water • The Trooper.
00699676 Book/CD Pack.............. $14.95

8. Punk Rock
Songs: Brain Stew • Buddy Holly • Dirty Little Secret • Fat Lip • Flavor of the Weak • Gotta Get Away • Lifestyles of the Rich and Famous • Man Overboard.
00699813 Book/CD Pack.............. $12.95

9. Blues
Songs: All Your Love (I Miss Loving) • Born Under a Bad Sign • I'm Tore Down • I'm Your Hoochie Coochie Man • Killing Floor • Pride and Joy • Sweet Home Chicago • The Thrill Is Gone.
00699817 Book/CD Pack.............. $12.95

10. Jimi Hendrix Smash Hits
Songs: All Along the Watchtower • Can You See Me? • Crosstown Traffic • Fire • Foxey Lady • Hey Joe • Manic Depression • Purple Haze • Red House • Remember • Stone Free • The Wind Cries Mary.
00699815 Book/CD Pack.............. $16.95

11. Country
Songs: Achy Breaky Heart (Don't Tell My Heart) • All My Ex's Live in Texas • Boot Scootin' Boogie • Chattahoochee • Guitars, Cadillacs • I Like It, I Love It • Should've Been a Cowboy • T-R-O-U-B-L-E.
00699818 Book/CD Pack.............. $12.95

13. Lennon & McCartney
Songs: All My Loving • Back in the U.S.S.R. • Day Tripper • Eight Days a Week • Get Back • I Saw Her Standing There • Nowhere Man • Paperback Writer.
00699816 .... $14.99

21. Rock Band – Modern Rock
Songs: Are You Gonna Be My Girl • Black Hole Sun • Creep • Dani California • In Bloom • Learn to Fly • Say It Ain't So • When You Were Young.
00700705 Book/CD Pack.............. $14.95

22. Rock Band – Classic Rock
Songs: Ballroom Blitz • Detroit Rock City • Don't Fear the Reaper • Gimme Shelter • Highway Star • Mississippi Queen • Suffragette City • Train Kept A-Rollin'.
00700706 Book/CD Pack.............. $14.95

23. Pink Floyd – Dark Side of The Moon
Songs: Any Colour You Like • Brain Damage • Breathe • Eclipse • Money • Time • Us and Them.
00700847 Book/CD Pack.............. $14.99

FOR MORE INFORMATION,
SEE YOUR LOCAL MUSIC DEALER,
OR WRITE TO:

HAL•LEONARD®
CORPORATION
7777 W. BLUEMOUND RD. P.O. BOX 13819
MILWAUKEE, WISCONSIN 53213

Visit Hal Leonard Online at **www.halleonard.com**

Prices, contents, and availability subject to change without notice.

0409